T0107817

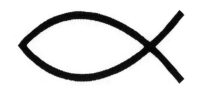

THE

TRIALS OF

A WOMAN

From Struggle to Survival

JOANN JONES

iUniverse, Inc.
Bloomington

The Trials of a Woman
From Struggle to Survival

Copyright © 2012 by JoAnn Jones.

All rights reserved. No part of this book may be used or reproduced by any means, graphic, electronic, or mechanical, including photocopying, recording, taping or by any information storage retrieval system without the written permission of the publisher except in the case of brief quotations embodied in critical articles and reviews.

iUniverse books may be ordered through booksellers or by contacting:

iUniverse
1663 Liberty Drive
Bloomington, IN 47403
www.iuniverse.com
1-800-Authors (1-800-288-4677)

Because of the dynamic nature of the Internet, any web addresses or links contained in this book may have changed since publication and may no longer be valid. The views expressed in this work are solely those of the author and do not necessarily reflect the views of the publisher, and the publisher hereby disclaims any responsibility for them.

Any people depicted in stock imagery provided by Thinkstock are models, and such images are being used for illustrative purposes only.
Certain stock imagery © Thinkstock.

ISBN: 978-1-4697-6095-7 (sc)
ISBN: 978-1-4697-6096-4 (ebk)

Printed in the United States of America

iUniverse rev. date: 03/07/2012

ACKNOWLEDGEMENT

This book is inspired by my Lord and Savior, Jesus Christ. First, I would like to thank God for allowing me to write this book. It was very difficult at first, but God and I finished it.

I also want to dedicate this book to my father Joseph Robinson Jr. (1948-1999).

I want everyone to know that my dad was a fighter. He was a good man. He instilled principles and God's teachings in our home. My father was a man of God. He believed the Bible completely. My father never gave up on anyone or anything he put his mind to. Joseph Robinson Jr. was full of perseverance and

because my father was such an inspiration in my life, I know that I too will never give up.

One scripture we heard often as we were growing up was, "Train up a child in the way he should go and when he is old he will not depart from it". (Proverbs 22:6)

That child was me and now I can truly tell everyone, God has changed me forever.

CHAPTER 1

TELLING IT LIKE IT IS

I was born in Greenville Mississippi, at a hospital called General Hospital. I was born to Joseph Robinson Jr. (1948-1999) and Eddie Mae Robinson Jones (1952-). There was a sudden silence when I was born. Upon arrival, my mother told the nurse when she saw me "take that boy back!"

The nurse replied, "Ms. Jones that's not a boy that is a little girl."

My mom insisted on not seeing me, because she was exhausted from giving birth to me. She said when she finally came to get me, I was bald headed and fat. The nurses were in amazement. My mom said, they had not seen a black baby born without hair on their head in a long time. My mom said, I came

into this world with clutching fists, ready to fight. She said my jaws were big and I had a mean look on my face. Well, as I grew into childhood, sho'nough I was challenged and fighting almost every day. I was never that child to bully people; I was the one that defended others from the bullies.

Someone had to stand up to those mean bullies, so I guess it had to be me. For example, in biblical days, there were people who stood up for good. David was a child when he slew the giant with a rock. God gives us courage to stand against our enemies and that is how I stood up to bullies.

I remember an incident when I was in second grade, everyday this one particular girl was being bullied by one of the meanest girls at school. I didn't know this little girl at the time, but I knew who the bully was. One day out of the clear blue, this girl

ran over to me as if I was the teacher. I know for a fact, when you are in trouble at school, you tell a teacher or an adult to help you solve the problem. This second grade girl ran up to me and was crying, yelling, and hiding behind me as if I was a shield of armor.

When I finally saw why she was crying and screaming, I wanted to run and hide. I thought, if I ran than this person was going to continue bullying other people. I was the typical second grader. I wasn't too heavy, but I was solid. This girl wasn't the typical second grader. The girl was, well to be truthful, she was big and bulky. From the looks of her, I knew that she had some strength. I walked up to her and stood directly in her face and said "If you want to pick on somebody, than pick on me!" "What if I don't want to pick on you," she replied. "Well you might as well pick on me," I said, "because you are

not going to touch or pick on anyone anymore." I kid you not, after all the second graders saw that, I was their hero. That bully never picked on anyone ever again. Actually, when we grew up, that bully and I became good friends. See, you do not have to accept things when they are wrong.

I use to do some things which were wrong, but God has forgiven me and told me to walk with Him. God has chosen me to speak to the world and let the people know, you don't have to do wrong. I was inspired by God to write this book, and share my personal experiences. In His words, He said, "If you follow me and obey my words, I will give you the desires of your heart."

It was a very big step for me to come back to Jesus again. I was scared and I was without any friends, no place to go and most of all I was tired

of being used and abused. I was so distraught and broken, I could have killed myself, but I thank God that I was not suicidal. No one knows what really goes on inside people's head when they are going through problems, only Jesus knows. During these hard times, if you do not have a strong support system to lean on, a person can be devoured. Look around people, our world is falling apart. My trials and tribulations were very massive. I encountered many dark paths. In this world there is a world war going on. But I tell you, the war inside of my head was greater than this world war.

See, I didn't trust anybody anymore, except Jesus Christ (My Lord and Savior) and my mom. When Jesus said "child come unto me, I will give you rest, peace of mind, and everything you need to survive." Yes, was my reply! The reason why I said

yes because first, I was raised in the church and second Jesus was my only way out.

What I'm telling everyone, there is a lesson that needs to be learned whether it is good or bad. You will have to learn that lesson, regardless of what it may be. In my situation, I use to do drugs and drink alcohol. I never had the desire to stop using drugs until I finally came to my senses. I said through the grace of God you will never control me ever again.

During my addiction, my drug of choice was crack cocaine. Crack is one of the most addicting drugs out there. If you really look at it, you are being controlled by a little white substance called "crack." Tell me how can crack control you? Well, let me tell you how. First, it becomes your god and it will tell you what to do. You can never get enough of it and the main purpose of crack is to destroy you. I know, because I was

on that road before. God has closed that chapter of my life. Sometimes, I wonder to myself, how did I let something so small control me?

People, I was serving another god. I wasn't serving Jesus Christ who died on the cross, shed His blood, and gave His life for me and you. I want to tell the world one thing about a phrase that isn't true at all and I want people to really stop believing this phrase, "once an addict always an addict." THAT IS THE MOST ABSURD PHRASE I HAVE EVER HEARD!!! Let me tell you why. They teach you in AAA meetings to accept that first. **DON'T DO IT!!!** When you accept God, He will make you forget that you ever did anything wrong. When Jesus frees you, you are free indeed. You just have to be strong and speak from experience. As for me, I am delivered from both drugs and alcohol.

For all people that are in doubt; God can do all things BUT fail. Hallelujah Jesus! God took me out of sinking sand and placed my feet on solid ground. He did it so easily. I felt like I was in Heaven. This is when I knew I was on my way to recovery. When I accepted Jesus back into my life and stopped doing wrong; the first thing God did was heal my mind and body so I wouldn't have any desires. Secondly, He restored me and made me a new person. God washed and cleansed me from all unrighteousness and sin.

To inspire anyone who is on drugs now, or has an alcohol problem, or any problem, Jesus will help you through it all. As for me, I didn't have to go to rehab and I didn't have AAA friends to talk to about my problems. I just had Jesus. I know some people need AAA to deal with their situation and this is alright. If it works, go for it, but I know from others

that went through AAA that the majority of them are repeat offenders. They still have the desires and they constantly fight the urge to use again.

Again I say, when Jesus frees you, you are free indeed. Jesus is all you need for any problem. Seek God and you will find Him.

A long time ago, on a still summer night, I almost lost my life. I was out late partying, doing drugs and drinking corn whiskey. I remember it so vividly. I was riding with two guys that night. One of them I knew, the other I didn't know. What I did not realize was their plan to rape and kill me. I told them to take me home, as we were approaching my place, they kept on driving. I told them they had passed my house. They did not respond, they just turned up the music really, really loud. I then watched them as they drove on a road that took us out of the city onto a country

road where you would find nothing but cornfields and an abandoned dusty road.

As we got to a certain area, I heard one of them whispering to one another "stop here", and the other said, "no keep going, we will find another place". Immediately, my defense mechanisms began to kick in as I thought about their intentions to kill me. I knew I had two advantages. First, my only chance of surviving was to use a corn whiskey bottle that I had in my hand as a weapon. Secondly, being in the back seat gave me the opportunity to take one out before the other one could reach back and shoot me. At this point, I want to tell everyone, most killers think before they commit the act and that is why I believe a person should get a more harsher sentence and should not be able to plead insanity.

I will never forget that night. I had that corn whiskey bottle in my hand and I told them if you all even think about killing me, one of you are going to go with me. By that time, I had a chance to come face to face with my killers. Unexpectedly, they changed their minds and started talking and fearing for their lives because now they didn't know which one was going to die with me. So they had a choice to make. They turned the car around and headed back into town. They stopped at the nearest gas station and told me to get out, "that girl is crazy!" I said no you all are crazy if you think that I was going to let you all take my life. I cried, prayed, and called my daddy after they let me go. I told my dad, I'm tired of running, doing wrong and being rebellious. It was time for me to surrender my life, whole heartily to God. Regardless of all my trials and tribulations during my addictions, God was watching over me.

I was married at that time with three children. I was doing the wrong things because I was trying to get out of an abusive and very dreadful marriage.

At that time, I was using drugs heavily. I remember one incident in which I needed another hit. I took the very last of my money and went out to buy some drugs. The person I bought them from said "I'm going to give you a good deal, since this is your last." When I got back to my place to smoke, my instinct told me to cook it up and I did. That poison popped all over me. He had given me toilet bowl cleaner. Truly I know, the last deal, he thought was going to be the death of me. See in the drug game, you don't have any friends. They don't care who they hurt. I heard a rapper say, they sell rocks to scum's and nobody's. See I'm not a nobody, I'm somebody. I was steered off the path and driven to the streets because of my abusive marriage.

My daddy and mom didn't do those things. I let peer pressure get to me. My friends always convinced me to use drugs and drink, they said to go ahead and try it, because it was nothing wrong with it. They said that if I try it you will find that you would really like it. Like Adam and Eve, when they ate of the forbidden fruit, their eyes were opened to every evil thing. That is how I was when I started doing drugs. My eyes were opened to all kinds of evil. I say to anyone who thinks they want to try something wrong or even want to do something wrong, think first. I guarantee your conscience will speak to you and say don't even think about it. When I first tried drugs I didn't' think at all I just did it. But if I could turn back the hands of time, I would have thought about it before I did it.

So this statement is especially for the younger generation. I know you are all exposed to everything these days; sex, drugs, lies, murder, etc. I'm here

to tell you young people, you only have one life to live. Once you die, it is over! You can't do what you want to do any more. Young people, I had a second chance at life and I am standing up and letting you all know, you each have choices in life. You can grow up and do the right thing or you can die at an early age and never have a chance to grow up. I changed my life for you all. I am pleading to the children, listen to your parents, they wouldn't steer you wrong, you will find out that you will grow up and live a much happy and longer life.

When I was a child, I was a tom-boy. I didn't play with dolls. I played with trucks, dirt, and other boys, so I could compete with them. I had to prove to them, I wasn't just a girl, I was a tom-boy and did what they did. When we were younger, we played like kids; we didn't grow up until it was our turn to be grown. Young people, it's not your fault why the

world is in such chaos. For the ones who will listen to me, and wait your turn to grow up, I promise you will be a very successful person and you will live a good and happy life.

I did take time to grow up, but I listened to my so-called friends telling me to do the wrong things. Let me tell you, I paid a huge price for it all. That is why I'm writing this book to you and letting you know that you don't have to accept wrong. For the children who are doing wrong, you might not have a second chance.

There is too much stuff in this world that is going on and it is time for the parents to stand up for what is right! Don't let your kids rule you; we must take our control back from them until they are of age. It is the fault of parents that have allowed the system to tell them what they can do with their own children.

I remember when I was young and everyone was allowed to discipline us. But now children you have taken advantage of the system and you have used it against your parents. Some of you need discipline and some of you just want to do what you want to do. But hold on, I promise each and every one of you who does not listen to your parents, you will suffer the consequences one day.

The Bible tells us in Ephesians 6:1 "Children obey your parents in the Lord, for this is right. Honor your Father and Mother, which is the first commandment with promise." I have heard many children say to their parents, "I wish you were dead!" How dare you say that to your parents! All of the children I affiliate with have respect for their parents now, because I'm telling them right from wrong. Listen and do good children, you all don't have a choice, when you're

with your parents obey and follow their rules. They only want the best for you.

I know I did things that I am not proud of, but now I don't make excuses for myself. I can't say at the time that I suffered like Jesus, because I didn't. I put myself through that shame. Just like slavery, once you free your mind from all wrong things and turn to Jesus you are free indeed. Did you know now the world is exposed to all kinds of evil devices? Back in the days television use to be something I loved to watch. Cartoons were my life. Cartoons are not cartoons any more. Now, they are too violent and demonic. Who made this play station, game boy, game cube, etc.? Get my point.

I remember when videos were something I wanted to play with and just have fun. Now children these days have videos where there is cursing, naked

women, and violence throughout its missions. The internet is a world-wide device that is used today to accomplish many forms of evil. I know you can use it for good, but now children can access things on the internet you wouldn't want to believe.

When I was a child my parents cared where I went, cared who I talked to, cared about me, period. Society has come in and told the parents they can't do that anymore. Basically, discipline your children.

Parents it is your fault that you accepted those things. You had a voice to speak out about things and you didn't. Parents, the world, we are all guilty for allowing our world to expose our children to all of this evil.

Last but not least, I target the schools. What happened to our schools? Who allowed someone to take Jesus out of the schools? That was the biggest

mistake this world allowed. I know that Jesus died for us. We hung Him on the Cross and He was innocent. I know we truly accept wrong doing. Instead of them picking Jesus for truth; the world told Pilate to give us Barabbas. We are all guilty in that cause unless we turn from our wicked ways and turn back to Jesus.

Jesus didn't come to destroy, He came to heal us, restore us, and save us for what is about to happen to this world of ours. To sum up everything I've said so far; don't ever make a deal with the devil or any one that is trying to steer you wrong. The devil will promise you something and then he will take it back. Eventually, he will kill you because you are serving him.

But I tell you this; God, Almighty God, gives you something He will never take it back. You see God is

everything which is good. He restores your life and leads you back to Him if you will just accept Him. He is ready to accept you. No matter what you've done, God is the only judge when it is all said and done. Wake up people! Remember how it use to be. Work hard and try with all your might to be heard. God will help you. "The Lord is my light and my salvation whom shall I fear. The Lord is the strength of my life; of whom shall I be afraid?" (Psalm 27:1)

Again you don't have to accept wrong no matter who you are or where you are at. I'm speaking to the world about all my trials and tribulations. I dedicate my life to God; to do whatever He wants me to do. I know I by myself cannot change the world, I'm just saying to the world, God is our only way out; surrender your life to Jesus. Jesus has the first word and the last word. Who will be able to stand and escape His wrath?

CHAPTER 2

TRIALS AND TRIBULATION

In this present time, life has many trials and tribulations that everyone must go through. Trials means a test and tribulation means something that causes suffering or distress. Everyone must go through a test of life, suffer and struggle through ups and downs, and God will help you along this journey.

My journey felt endless, like it was never going to be over. Until Jesus stepped in and helped me through my situations because I was so lost! I am a very observant person now and conscious of what is going on around me. I remember a while back, I was with my cousin and another guy, my cousin

proceeded to sell this guy some drugs. I'll never forget the words of warning my cousin told me that day.

"Do you see that guy?"

"Yeah"

"He looks normal doesn't he?"

"Yeah" I said.

"Well, always, always watch your surroundings. Always be alert. That guy has full blown AIDS. To look at the guy you would never have known. See my point, looks are very deceiving."

I was younger then, trying to learn the streets and observing everything. In order to tell a person anything you would have to walk in that persons shoes. There are a lot of people out here now perpetrating. They

really don't know the lives of a drug addict. They really don't know the lives of an alcoholic etc., unless they had a sneak peek of it themselves. Don't get me wrong there are people who have not walked in those shoes that can empathize with you, but only God gives them that gift.

Well, I had to experience it, hand-in-hand to really tell you what it does. In reality it destroys lives, families and everything you are trying to achieve out of life. It will leave you homeless, or dead. The whole purpose of me writing this book is to help you to understand and know that I just want to be a help to someone who is going through these things.

Some people will tell you to just give up. I am screaming at you, DON'T GIVE UP! Jesus is waiting with open arms to take you in. He is the answer to your problems, and He is the Savior of all who accept

Him. My reality was all about endurance; would one be able to hold out in this street game of drugs, lies, and deceit? I did and now I'm happier than ever. Walking with Jesus is truly joy unspeakable.

When I was a child I had it made. Even though I was ghetto-fabulous, I still had it made. My mom and dad took very good care of us. Sometimes we didn't know where our next meal was going to come from, but we always knew that daddy would provide some way, somehow.

I grew up with three other siblings. I have an older sister, Rochelle. She was the total opposite of me. She was a girly girl. She cared what people said about her and she cared about the clothes she wore. Most of all she wanted to be popular and she was. I looked up to my big sister for a while until I

realized I had to be who I was going to be. I couldn't pretend to be something I wasn't.

I also have a brother named Joseph. We called him "Red." He was totally for me, he imitated me. I was the tomboy so he use to do everything I did. I was a role model for him until he grew up and he realized too that he had to be who he was going to be.

Then last, but not least, I have a baby sister Josephine. We called her Josie. Now she wasn't the average child. She was my mom and dad's spy. We would have to pay her money not to tell on us when we did something wrong. Overall, she was the amazing one.

We also had another brother, who was our daddy's son, but not our mom's. Mom helped to raise him and Dad took care of him, but he didn't live with us. So each one of us grew up with our own

personalities. We loved each other, but we have had to take our own journey in life.

In life you have to make choices and you are the one who must make the decision. Which way are you going to go? It seems hard, but in reality it's not. I know if you are listening to right all the time, how can you go wrong?

I know there are some of you saying "how do you know what is right?" Well there is a little voice inside you that lets you know what is right or wrong. That is your conscience. Your conscience is your inner thoughts or feelings. Simple, right? Wrong! That is when choice comes into play. Will you do right or will you do wrong?

For example; a conscience speaks truth, but if it has been altered with drugs or alcohol, or anything which causes the mind to be clogged up or not clear

at that moment, you will not be able to make a clear choice. It will lead you the wrong way and in its path there will be destruction. That is why I say NO to drinking and driving and say NO to drugs.

How do I know that these things are no good for you? **Because I've done them**! I am telling you this from experience. I have no shame now, because I have turned a negative into a positive. With God on your side you can't go wrong. This book has a lot of topics, but I am writing to encourage others not to fall into the same traps I did. You can do anything if you have the mind to change and with God's guidance you will not fail.

Not everyone reading this is into drugs and/or alcohol, but there might be something you are doing. For example you might have hate in your heart. Hate is like a cancer that eats up all the good in you. It

could be something else. Maybe you constantly lie or you steal or you try to get others in trouble while making yourself look good. It could be any human weakness. In God's eyes one weakness or sin is the same as another. There is hope for each of us though, because God can turn your darkness into sunshine just as He did for me. I thank God every day for changing my life.

Now, I want to be able to help others to do the same thing. I have been through many trials and tribulations, ups and downs, rights and wrongs, and all of them have been a challenge. I ask each of you to stop and take heed to my words. Life is precious, you only get one life and it is too short to just throw it away.

Take a good look at your lives and see if you are on the right track. If you are not on the right track, get on the right track. Today is the day. Today you

are here and tomorrow you are gone. You know through all my struggles, I could have lost my life at any time. But I am a fighter! I knew I couldn't give up. I am a fighter, a soldier, a strong woman, and most of all I am a child of the King. When Jesus calls you and you accept Him, you will know you are His. He helps you to overcome anything and everything on this earth. We came into this world without thought and bad habits. I know if you have a mind to change, you can. Some people just wish they could change. Some people just talk about changing. Then there are those that know they can change if they put their minds to it and they actually do so. They change because they are fighters too.

Life is a struggle, it is a challenge, but you don't want to concentrate on the negative things. Concentrate on the positive things in your life. As soon as you focus your mind and heart on the

positive things, you will soon realize that you are somebody and you can do anything if you put your mind to it.

There is no reason for me to lie to you or to try and mislead you. My judgment, everyone's judgment comes from God. Some don't worry about that though; they are the types that will put you down regardless of the good in your life, or the positive changes you have made in your life. We call these people 'critics.' They are the kind of people that will tear you up and eat you for dinner.

One thing you should know is that some people talk bad regardless, so don't worry, it is ok. I have been there and I know of others that have been there and if we can make it, so can you.

As a woman, I have experienced a great deal. God has saved me and has brought me from death

back into life. I died so many times, I was a walking corpse. But God allowed me to come back to Him and I know He saved me for a reason. I am truly a miracle.

I know many people might say how could she go through those things? You might be one that thinks "she had a dad and mom who went to church and kept her on the right track, how did she let this happen?" Well, I did have church going parents, but on the other hand, I wanted to experience life my own way, not the way my parents were trying to teach me.

I can truly say I did made mistakes by not listening to my parents or doing as they tried to teach me. If I had listened to them, if I had done things as they said and took the advice they gave, I would not have

suffered like a did, but maybe, just maybe I would have had another set of problems to deal with.

In the end, I didn't listen to them because my heart was not in the right place with God. I was stubborn and wanted to do things my own way.

For whatever the reason, in a lot of ways, I am glad that I have been through what I have and I would like to share those reasons with you:

1) I have walked in their shoes

2) I am a living testimony

3) I have experienced good and bad

4) I have changed my life

5) I will succeed to the highest of my calling

6) I will be a helper and not a hindrance to society

7) I will stand for the truth

8) I shall not be moved by negativity

9) I shall obey the voice of God

10) I have overcome it!

I asked someone once "do they think they will ever stop doing drugs?" They told me they loved it. When I was doing drugs I loved it too. But if you really, really look at what you are doing it's really nothing. It is all in your head. It is just a habit you formed and became dependent upon. For example, when a baby becomes hungry it wants momma's breast, but if the baby couldn't depend on momma's breast, it would look or accept an alternative, like a baby's bottle. My point is if you take the drugs, alcohol, or other weakness away, you can't focus on the negative feeling that it leaves you with. The "oh no, now what" panic feeling.

You have to feel that void in your life with some positive realizations: 1. You will be able to live and

not die 2. You now have hope of a better life 3. If you turn to God, He will help you through it all and you will not be alone. I know a lot of you are saying "well I just don't think it can be that easy." I am not trying to tell you that it won't be a challenge, it will be, but a good life is worth fighting for. You are worth fighting for!

Many people today are altered in many ways. It can be just their plain stubbornness or being disobedient to those in authority. It does not always have to be drugs and alcohol related. When a parent or another authority figure in your life gives you instruction or asks you to do something, "why not just do it?" It is so easy to just listen to the positive influences around you.

Why are you trying to make things so difficult? Why are you allowing something to alter your

decision making abilities?" Comments like "you don't tell me what to do; I wish you were dead; or I hate you," those are harsh and disrespectful words to a parent or any adult. Please, you have to understand that we are only trying to help you. And often times we are trying to help you avoid making the same mistakes we did.

CHAPTER 3

LIFE'S JOURNEY

As you walk with me through the journey of my life, I will continue to tell you how I changed.

On this sunny day, thanking God for letting me live to see another day. I want to explain to you how I changed. Earlier, I told you all the things I have or may have done. Now I will tell you how I was converted and brought out of darkness, back into the light.

This chapter is a little like a horror movie. The difference is that this is not a horror movie, but the reality of my life as it was then. Do you know how it feels to be watched when you are not doing what you are suppose to be doing? That is how I felt

when I was in the streets. In the streets of drugs, lies, deception, and gangs. I want to take you all the way back to those times with me and share with you the other side of me.

My mom and dad had instilled good morals in me, but I wanted to experience life for myself. Not knowing that one day I would be writing about it. At nineteen, I dropped out of college. I wanted to experience the streets and do the things that I saw other people doing. It was then that I became a drug dealer. Selling drugs to people who I really thought needed them. I made a lot of money dealing drugs. It turned out, that life was too fast for me.

There were some that would come up to me and my crew and ask if they could get some drugs for free. I always told them no. Then they would be like "why?" They would say "please I'll get the money

to you when I get my welfare check or SSI." See I wasn't a heartless person, I had a heart, so in the end I would give them the drugs and tell them they could pay me later. I thought I was helping them, but now I know I was actually hurting them.

What made me so stressed and worried all the time was that people were taking their money and buying drugs, but they were not feeding their kids. They were doing whatever it took to get those drugs. My life was always a story book, but you could plainly see that I wasn't living the life of a fairy princess.

I peddled drugs for a little while longer. It was during my first pregnancy that I started thinking that it was time for me to get out of this thug and drug life. I never did drugs while I was pregnant, because I knew that I had to respect my unborn child. People

don't really understand that type of life unless they have walked in those shoes.

Growing up in the ghetto, you see it all and you have to be really strong not to get involved. Well, I was the one that made the choice to do the things I have done. A pastor told me, JoAnn you have so much to give, one day you will be a great teacher among the people. I did not know what he meant at the time, but God knew which direction I was going. He also knew I was going to endure so much and be able to triumph through it all.

I wanted to make a change in my life so I moved to Pennsylvania to live with my sister and her husband. While living there, I found out that my dad was going to die. That was when my nightmare started. My daddy often told me not to marry so young, but I did! When I did get married, I was so

unhappy and always seem to be looking for a way out.

I did get a chance to talk to him before his death. During our conversation he replied

"Are you alright?"

"Yes Dad. I'm not coming back down south until I make something out of myself."

I should have known something then when my Dad said he loved me. I knew he loved me, but he wasn't the kind of dad that usually told you those words. While thinking nothing about that, I started going places, doing what was right and seeking God for everything. One morning we got a call saying that dad had died. I had loved him so much, he always had my back. He never disowned me and nothing that I have done. We use to talk about everything.

Going back down south to bury my dad and see him for the last time was one of the most painful things I ever had to do. When he passed away I was so hurt. I started blaming everyone for his death including God. I started resenting everybody. I had hate in my heart and my heart was black. I thought my daddy's death was a tragedy even though he was with God and I knew he was in a better place. I started to drink heavy and drank until I didn't even know if I was coming or going. All I knew was to stay high, but through it all, it was a struggle and it took all of my heart. I had a heart, but it was hidden deep down inside.

Look at the real me now, stable, in shape, focused and loving God. Every step I make now I know that God takes it with me. When one is focusing on so many things in their lives, they don't have any time to think of all the good things in life, because they are so caught up on the things that are going wrong. A

person without knowledge is like a baby who doesn't have knowledge when they are born. I was always a wise person, but I was using it the wrong way. Now I can clearly see my future. The way it was going to be from the beginning before I was altered off the path. Now I'm here alive and well!

One day, I was working at a store waiting on a customer, when she was walking out she said, "once bad always bad." Don't believe that. Society wants you to accept certain things the way they want you to accept them. I'm here to tell you that God can turn a bad person into a good person. Look what He did for Apostle Paul. Apostle Paul was not only killing Christians, he thought he was right in doing what he was doing. God changed Apostle Paul and he became the greatest Apostle of his day. If you haven't read the Bible yet, READ IT. There is a wealth of information in God's Word for you. For all of us.

In this world people will judge you quicker than you can blink. The Word of God says in (Matthew 7:1) "don't judge least ye will be judged." I try not to judge anyone because only God has the final judgment. I know we have earthly judges, but they are here to keep justice. I'm saying there are many people out here that don't have hope for tomorrow and society has failed them. That is when the crime rate goes up, drugs are on the rise, and our prisons are becoming full, etc.

I thank God every day that I was never involved in the system. When I was in my drug use, I didn't need rehabilitation or a parole officer. Because I had my family, who was my strong support system that believed in me and most of all Jesus Christ, my Savior.

I thank God for that because without Him holding me I would be nothing. God knows why He

saved me and lifted me out of the dirt that I was in. I also remember when I stopped doing wrong and I started to travel. I met a man that told me to expand my horizon and that is what I did. My horizon is far beyond this world.

This world is so messed up, but I believe this world is mine through Jesus Christ. He said this is the promise land of His people and I believe it. Folks wake up! This is it! If you don't own something, own it now, this is our land. This is not man's world, this is God's world and nothing is going to happen to this world until God truly returns to get His people.

God says, He is here to show us the way and people are choosing wrong rather than right. I am telling you all about my trials and tribulations and holding nothing back. 1. I'm not ashamed of who I am 2. There was a lesson to learn 3. I'm doing the

right things now. Isn't that what REAL society wants? It wants you to stand up and change your life. Live for the truth and never fear anything or anyone but God Himself.

Life is no game; I learned that lesson the hard way because of the path I chose. If you have a problem and want to change than hold your head up high. You can do anything through Jesus Christ. Rise above it all and live. I thank God every day for allowing me a chance to live and not die before I made this miraculous change.

There are different types of spirits in the world right now and if you follow the wrong one you will perish. Before I was converted, demonic forces tried to tear me to pieces. One knows how piranhas will eat you alive. Well that is what they tried to do to me. But I will not be torn apart. I will stay whole till the

day I fall asleep in the Lord. I continue to talk about my change without rehabilitation. I was rehabilitated by Jesus Christ.

More and more I unfold a lot of secrets about myself. I want everyone to recognize and see themselves for who they really are inside and to dig deep inside and pull their selves up and out of the mud. Dust off and say thank you Jesus. I can do anything through Christ that strengthens me. If you think there isn't a lesson to be learned here think again, there is always a lesson that needs to be learned.

CHAPTER 4

<u>WHO I AM NOW</u>

This chapter will only talk about how my walk of life is now and continues to be. One day at a time. I would like to tell you to love yourself first before you can love anyone else. How can I love you if I don't love myself? One should want to change and stay changed until they leave this earth. I know there will be many people who will read this book and condemn it, its ok. There will be people who read this book and it will change their lives like I've changed mine.

Remember you don't have a lot of time, you have to make your decision now while you still have time. Time is short and life is precious. Choose this

day who you are going to serve. Good or Evil? I chose Good, why don't you? Like a wise man once said "just do it." You have to have a heart of a lion and don't be afraid to call Jesus out of the sincerity of your heart. He will rescue you. Hold your head up high, you could be here today and gone tomorrow. God is in control. I don't care who you are, God will always win.

My walk of life has always been a struggle, but yet I never gave up. I remember there were times when I just wanted to throw in the towel. There were many voices, telling me to just give up. But there was one voice that told me not to. So I listened to that voice of reason and I'm up and still running. There is a race each of us must run. The prize is not given to the one who starts the race, nor to the one that runs it the fastest. It is given to the one that finishes the race. Join me and let's finish the race together.

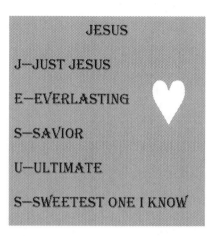

JESUS

J—JUST JESUS

E—EVERLASTING

S—SAVIOR

U—ULTIMATE

S—SWEETEST ONE I KNOW

I always considered myself to be quite unique, because I never wanted to be like anyone but myself. I guess that is why God saw fit to save me. There are so many people out there imitating other people and following in their steps. I say STOP! Don't get me wrong, there are good followers. I'm talking about kids looking for things and love in all the wrong places. For example; gangs, drugs, sex, deception. There are kids out there right now following those

examples. Either an individual or individuals drove these kids to these places. The pressure to follow was just too powerful for them.

Children, you don't have to follow in those steps. I am here to help you get on the right path and stay on the right path. I promise I will help as many young people as I possibly can. Anyone that is willing to change I will be by your side encouraging you every step of the way.

I will open up recreational places for you, I will hold group meetings and I will do everything in my power to help children to be children. To the parents that have allowed our children to go off the path of goodness, you will be judged to the ultimate. My Bible says it is better for you to have a millstone tied around your necks and buried in the depths of the sea. TV, radios, video games are destroying our children. Parents I

say again, "BE AWARE." God has something for each of you. Children shouldn't be exposed to these things because we weren't exposed. Give these children a chance to grow up and choose their own path. If television, video games, and radios are doing it for them, how can they have a chance?

Today, I have chosen to be a motivational speaker because someone somewhere needs to hear my story. There are people everywhere in every walk of life that need to hear my story. If it helps one person or two I know I've done my job of reviving another life back to Christ. Like I said before, if anyone wants me to come and share with them some of my personal experiences, I would be glad to stand up and tell the world. I realize that there are a lot of people that are not as fortunate as to tell their stories of survival. Either they didn't make it or

they have something that holds them back. I thank God that during my addiction I did not contract any type of illness or disease that could have taken me out of this world.

This day I'm HIV negative, drug-free, and I am as healthy as a bull. Thank God!!! I am truly blessed and one in a million. I know there are people who are HIV positive and still are using drugs. I say to you, there is help through Jesus Christ. The people that are HIV positive, I commend you for telling your stories of choosing to live and not die. I'm willing to go as far as I need to go to help my sisters and brothers all over the world. I've dedicated my life now to help society and not be a hindrance anymore. I also know I am loved by many people of all ages, all races, and all walks of life. I have been to many places with many people and I tell you, I aim to travel around this world.

There is one greater who foresees beyond the beyond, there is such a one that will see what you are doing before you do it. I know that is Jesus Christ.

I have said that life is a struggle and it is. Life is what you make it. Struggles will come, but for the most part if you stay strong, it will not last. Most people with problems want things to work out when they want them to, but that isn't going to happen. You have to at least put a little effort in it if you want to see some results.

Before, I didn't have a right mind to work out any problems because I was altered by all types of things. I'm glad, "I can see clearer now, the rain is gone and I can see all the obstacles in my way". That is a true song and it is so true in my life. There are many doors that were opened in my life. Whether

it was good or bad, these doors were unleashed to make me or break me. I have so many dreams that will become reality, I will open many positive doors, one can't even imagine.

These days and time life is very hard if you're not focusing on something positive in your life. I am so glad that I came to my senses before destruction. I realize that when you are not doing right you are walking through the valley of the shadow of death. Anything may happen to you without God. I say again I am a true miracle. It was a miraculous change. I am blessed from the top of my head to the bottom of my feet. If you are reading this book you too can be transformed and you will walk in the trueness of life.

This is my story, my life and I chose to tell it like it is. I remember when I first decided to write this

book I didn't believe I could do this. Now every time I write, I can see more light. Stand up for the truth if you really know the truth. Like society, society wants a person to prosper, but is that the truth? If a person changes their lives, will society accept it or will society not accept it? Statistics say no, but people can and do change. I say if you truly want to change, ten out of ten can change.

While studying psychology, I found that statistics said if you follow all the right guides with little or no failure you would be successful. Who will say you are right or wrong? What works for you might not work for me and what works for me might not work for you. I do know this, "every knee shall bow and every tongue confess that Jesus Christ is Lord, to the glory of God the Father." (Philippians 2:11). Jesus Christ is King and He is risen from the dead.

I have to say when I was in my addiction, I remembered going into people's houses to smoke or to drink and I remember them watching me day in and day out, just waiting for me to drop. But Praise God!!! I am still here!

Experience is a teacher, it will make you or destroy you. Disobedience will leave you left out and down in the dumps. I can tell you to listen to your heart. Hearts don't lie. Be strong and remember to always take one day at a time. Don't look back in your past. Keep it moving and look forward to a long and prosperous life.

CHAPTER 5

<u>LOTS OF TWISTS</u>

I will paint many pictures; there will be a lot of twists. I would like to say people love to have pictures in their heads all the time. If it is only so vivid, it still was painted. People love to make speculations about one another and I tell you they don't have to know you. They will just assume they know. I tell my children all the time not to assume anything. Assumption will get you in a whole lot of trouble.

If a person say they know you because they saw you one time, they're just speculating. In reality, they don't know you they are just assuming. How can I tell someone I know them if I wasn't raised with them or was friends with them for years? Let me open

your eyes to something. People use to tell me they knew me all the time, but I would say to them "how do you know me?" One might say because I went to school with you or maybe I see you around all the time. Come on! Those are not good reasons. You cannot judge a book by its cover. You have to have had contact with that person or have been raised with that person.

I'm telling you and I know everyone will agree with me; people are always trying to find out who you are. Like now, unless I tell you who I am you still wouldn't know. I am simply saying before you paint a picture, first get to know them and remember, **don't assume anything**.

I remember when I was growing up, people tried to figure me out or wonder what made me tick. I was always one step ahead of them. I don't know

why people want to invade other people's privacy. They try to figure you out, so that they can have the opportunity to sabotage your life with lies and deceit. Then you will hear, "I told you that person is not who you thought they were." People wake up!!! You know society has always put labels on people. Their labels basically consist of "that one's bad and that one's good." I want everyone to know that you can't label me.

You can try, but I already know who I am and there is nothing anyone can say to me or say about me that will make me doubt myself. There are people out there right now saying "she use to do drugs" and there are people saying "she beat the odds" and they are happy for me. I proudly say I have overcome! I am a person who God chose. I went through all these trials and tribulations just to

be a help to the next person that is going through what I went through.

Here is the twist. People say they are happy for you when you make a change in your life for the better. Take me for example, have people accepted me for everything I've endured or has society said once bad always bad. Don't believe what society says about you. Only one being can answer that and that is God. Ok, look at it like this, when you leave this earth there is only one of two places that you could end up going, Heaven or Hell.

If society fails you like they did me, who is greater than society? I was always a person who had love from my family. It was not that I wasn't loved, it was being accepted in society that was the problem. There are people that society has written them off from being accepted. Will I be accepted if I'm too fat? Ok,

look at Hollywood, why are they starving themselves to be thin? I think that is so wrong. A person should be accepted for who they are and not for how they look. I know if you are honest, a lot of you will agree with me. Why has society written us off? That's why I started doing wrong things, just to be accepted. I was wrong and look where it got me. I abused drugs and alcohol. I say to society, let a person be who they are to be, there is a reason for it.

People lose weight for a reason, all to say how they did it. A person stops doing drugs all to say how they stopped. I thought this is how its suppose to be. Learning from one another. All I want is to teach the world how to be a help to one another and prosper. I would also like to tell everyone you can have all the money, all the oil, everything you may possibly want in this world, but without GOD, it doesn't mean a thing!

Don't stop me from telling you how I've changed and how can I be a help to someone else. Isn't that what it is all about? It is about helping one another. I want everyone to know that I consider myself the least right now. You know what they say about the last. The last shall be what? The Bible tells us that the first shall be last and the last shall be first. (Matthew 19:30)

I study everyone like an experiment. You never know who is who until you uncover their true identity. During my first marriage, I was like an alien. A person that was not happy with the shell I was in. I had to dig down deep and pull out the real me. I know who I am now and I am happy where I am now. When God changes you, He transforms your mind, body, and spirit. In my past, my mind was like a maze, I didn't know which way to go. With perseverance, God has put me back on the right track, whole and

alert now. I tell you, if you are not on God's team you will perish throughout eternity.

I know there are some people that don't believe in God. For those of you that do not believe, search and you shall find. Someone is always going to see what you are doing and if you are doing anything wrong, you are not going to get away with it. The truth always prevails!

I know there are some people that had secrets and died. They went to their graves with it. Guess what? Someone else knew their secret before they died. God knows all, sees all, and is all which is good. My bones that I was trying to hide came back to haunt me and I just couldn't hold it in any longer. If there is anyone out there that has old bones in their closet, clean it out. I don't mean tell everyone. Whisper a little prayer and ask God to forgive you

and keep it moving. I know I can't touch everyone, but there might be someone that is listening to what I'm saying. Take heed so you won't perish, but have everlasting life with Him.

Tell me, who wouldn't want that promise from God. A promise to live everyday happy, peaceful, joyful, and clean. Why wouldn't you want that? I speak for myself when I say "I do want that" and that is why I have changed my life.

For those that personally know me, I will be that example for you and let you know people can change and be very successful. I say it is not easy, but all you have to do is take one day at a time. I don't know when I am leaving this world, nobody knows, so all I can say to you is live one day at a time and live good with all people. Be good to the best of your ability. If Jesus did it, we can too.

You have to have faith and put one foot in front of the other and keep moving.

I know there are so many negative people out in the world today, but don't follow them. Find a church or congregation of people that accept the truth and accept you for who you are. And when you have found the truth, change yourself for the better and take one step at a time.

It can be done!

Society only wants to accept what they want to accept, but I say that is wrong. They have written off the drug addicts, alcoholics, homeless people, hungry people, etc. Can someone please tell these people there is help? Don't turn your back on these people, lend a helping hand like it is suppose to be done. That is how Jesus wants it to be with no exceptions to the rule.

All I want is everyone to know that you only have this one life. I'm letting you know that whatever you've done on this earth before you leave, you will be judged, whether you've done good or bad. Why take a chance? All I'm saying is live good with everyone.

CHAPTER 6

KNOWLEDGE

In this day and time everyone must have some type of knowledge whether it is school, street, or knowledge from God. I prefer knowledge from God. He gave me knowledge of Him, but He also gave me a desire to go back to school and finish my education.

I attended a wonderful high school, T.L. Weston. I attended that school from 1989-1993. I have to acknowledge a few people here which, would be God first. And now, I would like to thank all the teachers that put up with me and helped me along the way. I had great teachers then, who would never let me give up. Also, I want to thank my one special

cousin that sat in class with me in the 12th grade, in order for me to graduate. I love you always.

I remembered when I almost dropped out of school in the tenth grade for a really dumb reason. At that time I thought it wasn't dumb, but looking back I realize it was dumb.

I had a friend, or at least I thought she was my friend. She was really a so-called friend. I say so-called friend because she put me through a lot of hurt and pain. Friends don't hurt you, they are suppose to love you, support you no matter what situation you're in. Some people take other peoples friendships for granted and don't deserve to be their friends, while others try to use and abuse their friendship. There are few people that will stick by you through thick and thin.

At the time my dad was very strict on me. What I mean about that, he was a Christian and stood for nothing but the truth. At sixteen years old, I've seen other teens doing lots of things which caught my eye. I started to rebel and wanted to do what I wanted to do. Well, my friend had a mom that let her do whatever she wanted. Her mom worked all the time and really wasn't at home much. When I didn't want to go to school, I just hung out at her house.

One day, I lied and told her and her mom that my dad was whipping me to death. I said that because I wanted them to be my family simply because her mom wasn't strict with her. I didn't know that they already had their own little plan cooking. They wanted me to go to a foster home and become a statistic. They told me they were moving to Texas and they were going to take me with them. At first, I was so excited. That is until they told me I wasn't

ever going to come back home. I would never see my family again. When I started to think about never seeing my family again, I knew I couldn't do it. I would miss them all too much.

One day unexpectedly, a social worker came to the school asking about the abuse at my home. The bad part about it, my dad was there too. My dad looked at me and asked me,

"When have I ever sexually abused you?"

I replied "what!"

I asked my dad who told him this. I told that social worker my dad never did a thing like that to me. She said someone called and told them that I was being sexually abused. I told her he whips me a lot, but my dad has never done a sick, perverted thing like that. Not thinking, I then asked my dad if he believed that

I would ever say anything that would disgrace him like that.

My dad said "do you have an idea who might of said something like that?"

I replied "yes my friend Beth."

My dad said "see, why can't you be good and just obey my rules. Don't worry, everything will be alright, because I love you."

I knew my dad loved me, but I was not use to hearing him say it. That was very special to hear those words. I started crying and my dad hugged me and I hugged my dad. I was rebelling because I wanted my daddy to tell me every now and then that he loved me.

Parents, I hope you realize that sometimes that is why your children act out. It is because they need

to hear you say "I love you." Tell your children that you care about them and that you only want the best for them.

As you have probably guessed, that social worker didn't get my dad for whipping me because discipline back then was ok. I don't know who said we can't discipline our children because that made us better. I'm still alive, it didn't kill me. I thank my dad for disciplining me, it only made me stronger.

Why did my so called friend tell these people that lie about my dad? I realized she wasn't my friend. If she went to that extreme to get me out of the house, no telling what else she would have done.

I was a rebellious child at times trying to leave home before my time. I strongly express to children all over the world, if you're not getting abused at home, stay there until it is your time to leave. Don't

rush things, I really learned an important lesson that woke me up, allowing me to get back on the right track and finish school. I told my dad that I would obey all his rules and stay in school and that is just what I did. I graduated from high school and received my diploma. Sometimes it takes something to happen drastically for a person to wake up, and sometimes it just takes a little more talking to.

For the children out there that are getting abused and can't be at home, find a counselor, a family member, or another adult that you know and trust. Please tell them what is going on. Don't be scared. Stand up because you do not deserve that kind of treatment. And let the rest of us pray that the system works well and fair for each of these children.

Each case needs to be looked at and these children need to be placed in the right homes. If there

is a family member that is stepping up to help, look at them first. That just might be the answer that this child needs. Family adopting family can sometimes be just the right answer. Please let us all try to do the right thing. We want our children to grow up right and be successful.

Remember, you all said the children are our future. I had another chance and it worked for me. Lets give them a chance too. My second chance gave me the opportunity to complete my dreams. I always wanted to finish college. I want everyone to know there are many opportunities out there, but it is up to you to go after it. There are some people that get chance after chance to do the right thing and they don't even have a clue what to do. Then there are others who will realize this is just what they hoped for.

I took the opportunity that came my way to become faithful to what I believe in and to accomplish the things I wanted before it was too late. I realize now that you only truly have one real chance to make everything right. I took life for granted sometimes. Only now, I wish I could have done everything the right way the first time around. I think if anyone deserves a chance to make everything right that will be me. I made it very hard on myself. I can tell everyone if you have an opportunity right now to make it all good, please do so. Remember that you must be sincere. It has to come from your heart.

I'm in college now, I feel I will finish and get my degree. I love people, all people, and I think I wouldn't have made it if it wasn't for some of the people I have met along the way. People that showed me love and told me that I could do it. They gave me encouragement and hope. These people

know who they are and to each of you I give my heartfelt thanks. Thanks for your support.

My children are a big reason for my success as well. They kept me going because it was them that I had to take care of. It was my children that inspired me the most. They depended on me and I had to do it for them. My children have offered to me some of the best words of encouragement I ever received from anyone; "mom, we love you, you are the best mom, we are so proud of you mom." There isn't a mother in the world that would not love to hear those words from their children.

Last but not least, I want to thank my husband for helping me see myself for who I really am. I am so glad that he didn't judge me for who I use to be. He told me, "baby if no one loves you, I love you." And I knew he meant every word. People just don't

come to their senses by themselves; it takes love. Love from the people close to you, your family, your friends, and most of all God.

I hope everyone who reads this knows, it takes the world to come together as one, so that we can help each and every one that needs help. We do this so that they too can say they have walked in those shoes and then they can tell someone else their story and help them to continue. I know critics are saying it can't be done, but little do they know they need help themselves. If they take a little time out and focus on some of their own skeletons, they will find they too need to clean out their closets as well. Don't be so negative. There wouldn't have to be critics if we all just kept a positive attitude. I know, who am I trying to kid. There will always be critics.

Friends, the life I'm living now is so peaceful. I try always to keep my head up so I can always see what is coming my way. When people tell you there is no hope, you tell them they are wrong. As long as you have breath in your bodies there is HOPE. Thank God!!!

While attending school, I have faith that this time I will finish. I am determined to make this right. I have told my children to, "NEVER GIVE UP and ALWAYS follow your dreams. You can make them come true."

How about you? Have you ever wanted something so bad and maybe somewhere in the past, when you tried to realize your dream, you really weren't given a fair opportunity? I know that I was born to be an achiever and to make something out of my life. I'm a little older and wiser now. I know that if you are

honest and you work hard, you can have anything you want. I am continuing on now where I left off. I will continue to strive to do my best always. It is my goal to make my dreams come true.

My children do well in school and I see their willingness to learn. I pray they can see that in their mother too. I long for my chance to show everyone that if I can do it then you can do it too. May God bless the world, that one day we will be able to understand who we really are.

CHAPTER 7

CHANGE

How can a person change? First, I would like to say for God so loved the world that He gave His only begotten Son; whosoever believes in Him should not perish, but have everlasting life. (John 3:16)

Everyone has something or another they believe in whether it's good or bad. When people realize in their minds and really look at the picture, you can't change by yourself it takes some help; whether it's counseling, rehab, Jesus etc. You can't do it by yourself, you always need someone. I preferred Jesus because He gave His life for me and what better spiritual pureness that can be? Even if you had a little counseling in your life, don't get me

wrong, we all need a little of that every now and again. If you just sit down and talk to someone about your problem, you will feel better, realizing there is someone who is willing to listen to you. You might not go and do what you were going to do in the first place.

We need people who are sincerely a listener and not always a talker. I know if I had someone to listen to me then, I probably wouldn't have done the things I did. People say they care, but they really don't. "They say I hear you," but in the back of their minds they are saying, I have my own problems. Well think for a minute, whatever that person tells you might be a help to your situation also. It might help you not to make a mistake. That's why I tell you to listen and open up your ears to them and see what they have to say. It might be good and it might not, but sure you can always learn something from it.

One: Children have something to say, so listen to them when they are speaking, it might be a clue in telling you they need help.

Second: A humble attitude. A person is willing to except when they are wrong. Stay calm when you are talking and explain to whomever you are talking to. I need help!

Third: Accepting you are not right, and that you do want to change, you have to be willing.

Fourth: Prayer changes things; at least that's how I was raised. Pray to God that you want Him to come into your life and heal you from all the wrong things you have done. Don't just pray with your mouth, pray with your heart.

What I mean is, if you are sincere and you are ready to change your life you will see it plain and

clear. I remember when I was doing wrong; one thing I couldn't do to save my soul was to face myself. I couldn't look in a mirror. I knew if I looked into that mirror I wasn't going to see my twin. Instead, I saw another person, a stranger, which was not me. Now, when I look into a mirror, I proudly see the real me. I love what I see. Another thing, test what I'm saying is true. Look in a mirror, really look, who do you see? Do you see a beautiful twin of yourself or do you see a stranger which is not you? If your answer is a stranger, let me tell you another story and then I will tell you what to do to make that stranger disappear.

This section is for anyone who is battling with something or someone in your lives. It could be something such as drugs, alcohol, cheaters, liars, or something as simple as eating.

One day, I came home drunk and disoriented. I was very disgusted because I spent all my money. I began to cry very heavily hoping I could find a solution, for what I caused. I began to pray profusely prayer after prayer. At that time, I was like a vampire, I didn't like mirrors. I started to move closer and closer to the mirror, I wanted to see who was doing these thing to me. I eventually looked at myself and surprising to say, it was a scary sight. I covered my face with my hands and proceeded to leave again; but something wanted me to take a real good look at who that person was. I looked again and do you all want to really know what I saw in the mirror that day? I saw a person, no, it wasn't a person it was a thing that was inside of me. It had red eyes, fangs and tentacles in his head. I tell you that scared me to death. When I called what it was, which was the devil, I cried with a loud voice, Oh Lord my God,

I need you and then I started quoting scriptures. You know when Jesus showed up, the devil had to flee. Still looking in the mirror, I seen this with my own eyes, my reflection changed before me. I saw that monster tremble. When I saw that, I realized that God was all power. He sent him (Satan) back to hell from whence he came and I never had that experience again.

Your reflection can show you who you really are. If you see the same thing in the mirror and nothing changes you might be ok, but if you look in the mirror and don't see your twin here's what you do. You know the devil is possessing so many people these days and times, but if you follow these steps you can send him back on the fiery trail, back to hell!

One: You must have the courage to look in a mirror, he might be hiding deep inside you; if you really look you can see him.

Two: Confess to God, I don't want to do wrong anymore, tell the devil I plead the blood of Jesus Christ against you and ask God to make him disappear. People that know the Word of God know what I'm talking about and if you don't, you have to read God's word to find out. You have to speak it with authority and really mean it. He then will heal and save you from all evil. You must obey and follow Christ forever. I'm writing because I know what's about to come. This world is experiencing war in many places. One day, you will look and see Jesus on that cloud; it will be too late if you are not ready. People wake up and take control of your lives and realize Jesus is the only one who can save you. I realized through all my trials, I am serving God

forever. I owe Him my life and I'm now dedicated to Him. I hope my stories will help someone so that they will not go down that rocky road just as I did.

People in everyday life also have stories to tell, I want to be very successful in everything I do. They say the truth is the light. If someone wants to change they need to change their mindset.

Many people hearts are not right, or they are not honest with themselves. I tell you, forget about what you use to do and focus on what you want to do. Speak the words and it will come into existence. Then, give up all the old habits or ways and start looking for positive people in your lives. Knowing that you always have a choice, there is only two choices you have to make, good or bad. I pray that you choose good. Look around you and know that this world is not getting any better, but you can get

better and change your settings, meaning move if you have to. Run and don't look back, but remember never forget where you came from. By remembering that, you will not want to go back to where you came from. People sometimes have problems, but don't think their problems through entirely. You don't have to result to drugs, alcohol, etc. If you really think about it, problems don't always last they come and go. If you can remember it's only a test to see if you will hold out or hold on until you see some sunlight. At that time, I didn't know if I was coming or going; things clouded my mind. What kept me was my endurance, my will to live a longer life. I know there might be someone who wants to end your life. **DON'T DO IT!!!!** When you take your own life; there's no coming back, you will never see the light of day ever again.

Life is precious; live your life like it's your last and do **Good**. One day you are going to leave this world. Pray that God will forgive us and save us to be His children.

CHAPTER 8

GOD IS LOVE

This chapter will reflect accordingly:

L—Life O—Obedient V—Victory E—Everlasting

When you test this, what type of LOVE do you really have? Let me tell everyone what kind of love I had before and what kind of love I have now. Back then, when I was young I use to love my friends and in return they hated me. I use to share my food with them; they would eat with me and afterward talk about me. I use to let my friends play with my toys and they would purposely break them or say they lost it. I didn't understand back then how kids could be so cruel. When I went on the school bus, I

wanted to sit down, but they always told me the seat was taken even though it was empty. That is some of the obstacles I endured.

I always got challenged in everything I did. I didn't understand it quite well, but I knew there was someone always there waiting to catch my tears. I had to play rough and tough as a child or the other children would run over me. Even though I always had a heart of gold, I would give children my last; I guess God always had a hand on me.

When I was about eleven years old, there was a boy bully in our neighborhood. He was never like that at first; people use to pick on him a lot until he became a bully. Well, my sister and I was trying to go pass him one day to go through this dead end that leads to another street. He told us that he was not going to let us pass unless we fight him. My sister

was thirteen at the time, she and I were very scared, but someone had to stand up to him. I started to play like I was really crazy, I started jumping up and down screaming and telling him that he better move out of our way and let us pass or else! He started getting really scared and told me; "you are really crazy" and he let us pass.

At that moment, I had to do something scary than him. I had love for my sister and I felt that I had to do something although she was older than me. My love back then as a child was very strong. People use to say how sweet I was, but I couldn't show love all the time, I had to be hard core. If people see your weakness, they will use it against you.

Now that I am grown, people really take my kindness for weakness. I've changed now, I can take more. I hope someone can relate to me and know it is

the love of God that keeps us. Love is very powerful, it was said that we have to love one another in order for love to return unto you. Love conquers all.

In these present times, people do not want love, they want to judge you, to tell you how worthless you are and that you will not accomplish anything. I don't know why people do the things they do, I guess it is because they really do not want you to have anything or anyone to love.

People think just because they have the finest things in life, they can say or do whatever they want. I am here to say that they cannot. It does not matter what you have, but it does matter how you treat and talk to one another. People must always say kind words to one another. Who knows what that person is going through!

I remember one time someone told me that they wanted to kill themselves because they did not want to be abused anymore. I told them that things happen for a reason. It will make you stronger or you will eventually follow through with the plan of taking your life. I told that person that God created them for a reason; not to go through abuse like that, but to be here to tell someone else what they went through so that it may be of help to others.

I want to know what makes people do what they do and say what they say. I always gave people advice and I have always been a listener to know how to deal with that problem. I guess I had enough love inside of me to step back from that edge and be who I really was going to be in the first place. You only pass through this world once, and if you give up and do something stupid, you will not get another chance to correct it.

Young people, your parents love you. I am speaking to the parents that raised their children to be all he or she can be. If your parents are crying out for help for you, it is a reason for it. Let them help you. You might even think that you don't need their help, but parents know best.

Young people open your eyes and see that this world is in chaos and it will destroy you if you allow it. I know there are children right now who wish that they have good parents like yours, but all you want to do is create bigger problems for your parents. I know there are children who wish they had a good home like yours and they do not have anywhere to live. What is wrong with you children? Why would you run away from home especially when you have parents and everything you need? Who does not want that? There was no need for me to act that way when I was younger, because I had two good

parents and we did not have much, but we had everything that we needed.

I cry out to all of you because all you have to do is wait your turn to grow up. I know there are children as young as ten years old on the streets and I pray that one day, God will put everything into perspective.

Children sometimes go on the streets and prostitute their bodies to get drugs and alcohol, because some of them are disobedient. Things like that happen when you do not want to listen to adults who are willing to give you all the love they possibly can. I know it's going to take a lot of love to bring you back. I have a lot of children who look up to me and I can't let them down. I let them know I've changed my life because of them. In the community where I live, I throw parties for the youth, dance contest,

cookouts, fundraisers, motivational teachings, and tell them about Jesus, and most of all, I love them all through Jesus Christ. I want to meet as many children in the world from every race. If I can, I would love to be their mentor through buddy letters. Since I've changed my life, I will always be Jo Ann Jones, a person that loves God, and loves God's people.

I love myself and most of all love the children of this world. God will protect me, even when people try to turn my good into something bad. Don't judge my future because of my past. It's not what I did; it is what I'm doing now. I want the world to know it's my time to shine!

Love is like a river, it will never stop flowing. My heart is overflowing with love. I would love to share it with people, I show them how to love and treat people as God wants them to be treated. Where I

work, people ask about me all the time. If I'm not there, they want to know when I will be back. It's just like I'm their sunshine. They say they are very happy when they see me, and little as they know, I am happy to see them, because they make my day.

I looked up the word "love" and it has many meanings. I chose this definition: "Love is a deep and tender feeling of affection for or attachment or devotion to a person or something." My definition of love is God. He truly loves us, because He gave us His only begotten Son, who died on the cross for us so that we might have life and more abundantly.

Tell me who would give their son for us? I tell you no one. I ask everyone to examine themselves; reconstruct your life. If you don't have love, put love in your heart, we all know you can't get to Heaven

with hate in your heart. If you want to be loved, ask God to open your heart and give you love so you can love someone else. Before you love someone else, you have to love yourself. And for those that hate purposely, I hurt for you, it's your problem not ours. As I close, tell someone of another race you love them. It's a start. May God be with you all at the end; He will have the first and the last word.

Chapter 9

VICTORY

This chapter will discuss victory. I say you may try to strip me of my dignity and pride, but you can't take my victory *for it is mine!* I had to go through so many trials, many decisions, and most of all hurt. I endured pain, struggles, trials and tribulations. This is my testimony; I can't let the struggle of life go unheard. My struggles were tough. They were not by chance, but by choice. I made many decisions, I had to reason, learn, and walk the right way. I wasn't always doing wrong. I still continued to study in school; I worked, went to church, read my Bible and prayed as I am still currently doing.

I was a very adventurous person in the streets. I wanted to get that street knowledge, at least that's what I wanted at first. I found out the hard way, why you should keep your nose out of other people business. Once you know something, you know it for a long time. Especially, when it was something you saw that gave you an interest, if it was not something positive, it can lead you down a very dark, gloomy, and rocky road.

One day, my fiancé, who is now my husband and I was driving out of town and the car broke down in the middle of nowhere. It was pitch dark and there was no light to be seen unless a car passed us by. We got out of the car and began to walk. As each car passed us giving us enough light to see an upcoming exit. I said "let's take the exit", he said no let's keep walking and eventually we are going to make it to our destination. We had about another

10 or 11 more miles. I was just thinking about that long walk.

Anyway, after exiting off the highway, I saw nothing but pure darkness. As we were walking I began to think that maybe he's right, we should have stayed on the highway, but I didn't let him no yet that he was right. We just kept on walking. By now, we had been walking for two hours on the wrong road. We had to climb this big hill and I look up and said, "man, I'm about to camp out here! I can't go any further". He replied, "you got us in this mess, and you are going to keep moving". I said okay as I proceeded to walk up the monstrous hill. I put all my strength in it, and kept it moving.

We then spotted a gas station, when we went inside this guy directed us to take a certain road which will lead us back to the right road. We then

went on and were back on the right road again, until the street eventually ended. Oh no! what's next I said? Which way should we go. The guy at the gas station only gave us part of the directions. He did not say that we would run into a dead end and where to go from there.

Now we are lost again. We are looking and debating, mind you, there is no light in sight. Two ways to go right or left. I told him "I'm going to let you pick this time", I pick the wrong way the first time. So he did. He made the right choice. By this time, it was about 4:30 a.m. Our car broke down about 10:00 p.m. that night. We had been walking for approximately 6 1/2 hours. It was a good thing it was summertime, I probably would have frozen to death if it was winter. When they would have finally found me, I probably would freeze into a statue standing straight up like the Statue of Liberty.

We now had one more mile to go. We made one final stop and got something to eat before we made it home. Before I crash and went to sleep, I had to thank God for helping us to make it home safely. I know that journey was for a reason. Though looking back now at that time, I believe it was a test of our faith. Faith means something. God says if we have faith as a grain of mustard seed, we can move mountains. I walk by faith and not by sight. If I look at these things, I realize that nothing is impossible for me to overcome.

Here is another story. One day, I just got my pay check, it was a Friday. I'll never forget when I almost lost my life again for the third time, at the hands of my so-called friends. I must have had about twelve hundred dollars on me, I said I will go and purchase some drugs first; then I will go home and later, get dressed and come back out when darkness falls.

I was at this house with my so-called friends. They lived a perfect normal life at least, that is what I thought. Their house was beautiful, but they had a secret life. In their basement is where all the wrong took place. I called this guy, one of my boys to come and serve me "crack" that I purchased. I figured no one was going to be greedy, so I was going to sell what I was going to sell to make my money back and afterwards do some myself. I paid them not to let anyone inside of the house, but as soon as the transaction had taken place, I noticed people started to appear from nowhere.

Even then, I had a spiritual ear to know when I was in danger. They had two daughters that did drugs as well as themselves. One daughter was good, but the other one was wicked. The wicked daughter convinced her mom to rob and kill me. My so-called friend agreed to it; I heard the guy with the

gun say, "when the lights go out nobody don't know what happened."

That's when I hurried up the stairs and called my oldest sister. If I was going to die at least, I would have left a message with my sister. I called my sister, but surprised to say, she wasn't at home at the time. I left a message on her answering machine. I told her where I was, left the address of the house, told her the name of the person.

By then, the wicked daughter ran upstairs and tried to stop my phone call, but it was too late. She yelled out to the others downstairs, "cancel that she made a phone call". The homeboy that I made my transaction with, he came and got me immediately. He was there in seconds and he came bustling through the door, threw me a gun and I got all my drugs out and we got out that house like true westerners gunfighters.

I want the youth to know, there is only but one perfect love and everything else is not good. Young people, there is no exception to the rule for you all. You all have to learn the straight and narrow path. I know there are going to be some young people that are going to listen to me and receive all the blessing in life or be hospitalized, by following the wrong crowd, or dead. I didn't lose my life, but I felt like I did. I was following behind the wrong crowd.

Victory in Jesus is mine! I thrive to be the best I can be. All you have to do is be yourself. Don't be in such a hurry to grow up. Learn all you can at home and then when it's your time to leave the nest, at least you would have some type of knowledge and wisdom how to grow up and make something out of yourselves.

It is not God's will for anyone to perish, but you have to choose which path to take. The devil is always out lurking, trying to deceive anybody he can. Be careful, Satan will deprive you if you make a deal with him. God help you, you are already dead. Satan always takes back his deals. He's a perpetrator, wicked, and don't care anything about you. Be aware of his tricks. Do not fall short before you find all of God's goodness that He has for you. All I'm saying, there is a God and He is greater than anyone and anything in this world. Please take heed to what I'm saying. For God so love the world that He gave His only begotten Son that whosoever believes in Him should not perish, but have everlasting life (John 3:16).

Victory is mine! It will be with me to the end of time. I know when I am sleeping; I have angels all around me protecting me. How I know they are there,

because God said so. One more thing, before you walk that dark path, stop, listen, and think. You will hear your conscience tell you wrong move. Listen people it's a warning from God. If you don't listen, it will take you down a long destructive road like I went.

I thank God that, He knew I was not going to self-destruct. He shone His light on me and put me back on the right path. I am a motivational speaker; I talk to as many people that possibly will listen. I do know the lives of people that are going through trials and tribulations and I will help as many of them that need help through Jesus Christ. Yes, I truly can say I have walked in the shadow of death. I know only God can save us when it's all said and done.

I kept getting knocked down left and right, I realized I wasn't on the right side. I was on weak

ground. Now, I stand on a solid rock, unmovable and strong. The story I presented earlier is an example of how dark your life can be if you don't have Jesus.

I don't understand how people can acknowledge so many things, but can't acknowledge my Savior and Lord Jesus Christ. He shed His precious blood for us, and He cried many tears. You all can at least know it's Him when He saves you from something bad. I watched a television show and on that show I saw a person fall from a twenty foot building, and the only thing he broke was his feet; don't tell me that is not a miracle! It's Jesus! People, He sends His angels to protect us.

Wake up world! Look up God is coming back and there is nothing you can do about it.

Hell is everlasting, it's hot and you can't ever say give me water. You will never get it. You will

burn every day, all day, everlasting. Do you want that? I speak for myself, "No way"! Hell is going to be everlasting and Jesus is going to be everlasting. Which one are you going to pick? I know there are people who don't believe in hell or heaven, I say to you, believe because it's true, you will one day soon see if its truth. Don't wait to late, pick Heaven.

Some people don't believe in God or the devil. Well, I tell you my God is ever alive and He shielded me through the bad times. Some people say it's a coincidence when two trains collide, yeah right. That is not suppose to happen, oh! yes it did. The devil wants souls also, and if he can steal a few by letting two trains collide, and so he will if you don't have Jesus.

You have to reconstruct your mind and evaluate yourselves daily. Reconstructing your mind means

knowing you've done wrong and knowing you can't look back in the past. Look forward always and take one day at a time that God gives us to make all our wrongs, right. Stay positive and love yourselves enough to want to change and make a better life for you and except nothing less but goodness. Stay focused on what you want the world to know and who you have become. I love God and I shall walk with Him. Victory is mine through Jesus Christ!

Chapter 10

THE FINAL ANALYSIS

Who the world sees you as should reflect the life you are living? Some people is always looking for the bad in people, some look for the good. Some can't accept that a person has changed only because they have some skeletons in their closet. I want to say there is no such thing as "There is no God". One must know God. I know because, I was that person living a dark and sinful life! God came into my heart to live and thrive with me so that I won't fall. I have endured a lot of pain and I have walked through many dark roads, but God has brought me out of each and every one of them and now I can walk in newness of life. I hope to gain in which direction my life is heading next. I have many endeavors to talk

to the world, and share my story with people all over. People always say "always follow your dreams". I have chosen to walk that straight path through my suffering and shame. I thought I wasn't going to make it, but I always had faith that one day things would get better. I want to be that miracle that says, lets keep changing together. Imagine this, when Jesus appears, and comes back for His people, all the people will be one. If people can't live in this world together, don't even think you're going to Heaven.

I don't beat around the bush; I tell it like it is. What profit is there by lying? There are people saying, I know I'm going to hell, but guess what, you don't have to go and this is how you will not go. Repent of your sins, and be baptized in the name of Jesus Christ and you can know Jesus for yourself. I realize now how important life is, only then was I playing with my life. A person only has but so much

time in this life, meaning you do not know when you're going to die. You're here today, and tomorrow you're gone.

In these days and time, you are remembered for so long, and then you are forgotten. Unlike Jesus, He is always remembered. He is the greatest of all time! How can a man come into this world over 2000 years ago, came to redeem us, and carry everyone's sin upon His shoulders. Receiving stripes upon His body, then get nailed to a cross, and die for us that we can have a chance to live again forever. People you don't have much time, if you are going to change your life, do it now. I am speaking to talk show hosts, radio hosts, Christian ministers, children of the world in every creed, color, and ethnic background, man, woman, everyone in the world, it's time to change your life, before it's

too late. For those of you that don't believe, keep on doing what you are doing. God will take care of you. For the believers take heed, watch and be ready when the trumpet sounds!

Parents teach your children right from wrong. Don't let them do what they want to do. Don't let society tell you how to raise your children. Parents, you are responsible for your children and your own actions. What about God's word? What if society told us, we can't worship Jesus anymore, will you listen? The answer to that is yes! You all will stop worshipping Jesus, if you all accepted that fact that society has told us we can't spank our children, we will be punished. That's backwards people! It says if you don't discipline your child, the parents will be punished, that's the truth. Test what I'm saying it is the truth, just look at the internet, how in the

world kids are in cyberspace. Who put them there, parents? When parents tell their children what to do and the child rebels and tells the parents you do it. Who has allowed our children to stray away? Parents, you all need to take control back from your children. Tell them we are not going to accept their wrong doing anymore. They are not going to talk back and they will respect and do what we say.

Another Issue—Teen pregnancies on the rise. Who has allowed our precious babies to lie down, and give away their innocence? They don't have time to be children anymore because they are making adult decisions before time. They are making their parents, grandparents before time. How dare society tell me how to raise my child, because I know what is best for my children. Society didn't care when I was straying off the path. They did not care where my children were. They did want to make

my family another statistic. Society doesn't allow the right resources to thrive and not be a statistic. Stop making people statistics and do something about why it is what it is.

When I start my journeys, I will tell you "why" why it is what it is. Stop the madness people, you will be held accountable for all your statistics. Does everyone know that we are suppose to be one people all over the world? Why are we fighting? Why are we suffering?

People are not making the effort to at least consider what the truth is. If a person really wants to know the truth. Read Matthew 7:7 "Ask and it shall be given to you, seek and ye shall find knock and it shall be opened unto you". For those that don't want to know, it is not our problem, it's yours. But for those who do, start reading your Bible, you will find Jesus

in the Bible. He will pick you up out of the dirt you are in and He will continue to dwell with you every day you are on this earth. He will be with you forever.

Trust Him, He is the key. Don't doubt God. Whatever He says He will do!!! It may take long, it might not, but He will do it every time. Take it slow and pray always. I'm going to say it's not going to always be easy, but don't give up. I say it again, do not give up!

People everywhere want to know who is "JoAnn Jones". Well, I will now tell you. I am a survivor. I was suppose to be dead, but I have an Almighty God I serve that said you are going to live my child. I have a work for you to do. Here I am in the flesh writing to everyone. I had to take heed to my life or I was going to be consumed. I had to change my life,

because I want to be that walking miracle that I was suppose to be from the beginning. What you see now is what you get.

I considered myself a positive role model in society. I am a motivational speaker, I am also a born again Christian, Jesus is the author and finisher of my faith. I have overcome my past and I look forward everyday to a brighter future. I can't speak negative about anyone because my bible tells me "judge not that you be not judged". That means, whenever you try to judge a person, or whatever it may be; what kind of judgment do you think you are going to get?

To make it simpler, when you are judging someone, you are judging your own self and not that person. I tell you don't do it! You will open the closet door to many skeletons. Sometimes I wonder, how can I handle the guilt of my past or how do I

deal with the shame? I will tell you how. God don't want us when we are perfect, He wants to be able to take us as we are. That's God! He wants to cleanse us Himself because no matter what, we cannot do it ourselves. This is how you can work towards perfection in Him!

As I stand tall today, God has shielded me and molded me into the person He wants me to be. I am more than a conqueror. I am who I am, just JoAnn. I keep it plain and simple. Before, I did not have hope, but today, I have hope in Christ Jesus. I know now that I have a future. I hope and pray that you do not judge me because of my past. I hope I have inspired someone to change. This book will help you along your journey.

I wrote this book with blood, sweat, and many tears. Speaking of tears, every time I cry now, I cry

with joy. I don't worry anymore because I know who I am. I am a winner. Why? Because I finally walked on a straight and narrow path. May the blood of Jesus always cover me, which I may continue to work for Jesus each and every day. I love each and every one of you. I forgive everyone that use and abuse me. Let love reign forever and ever. Amen!

As I end this book" I am woman hear me roar" may God be with us all and I pray God will save you before it is too late. May peace be with you! Hallelujah! Praise his name. His name is Jesus and He will reign forever. Take heed to yourself and change before it is too late. Do not tarry, for the Lord is coming soon and it will be too late. I say again change, before it is too late!

The moral of this story is ***MY WILL TO LIVE!***